MISSION WORK

Mission Work

Aaron Baker

A Mariner Original / Houghton Mifflin Company
BOSTON / NEW YORK / 2008

For information about permission to reproduce
selections from this book, write to Permissions,
Houghton Mifflin Company, 215 Park Avenue South,
New York, New York 10003.

www.houghtonmifflinbooks.com

Library of Congress Cataloging-in-Publication Data
Baker, Aaron, date.
   Mission work : poems / Aaron Baker.
      p. cm.
   ISBN-13: 978-0-618-98267-7
   ISBN-10: 0-618-98267-1
   I. Title.
   PS3602.A583M57 2008
   811'.6 — dc22   2007041925

Book design by Melissa Lotfy

Printed in the United States of America

EB-L 10 9 8 7 6 5 4 3 2 1

Grateful acknowledgment is made to the editors of the following jour-
nals in which these poems, some in slightly different form,
have appeared or are forthcoming:
Mantis: "Darkness Legend" and "Sing-sing Kiama"
New England Review: "Above Kerowagi" and "Spirits of the
      Low Ground"
Poetry: "Chimbu Wedding" (reprinted on *Poetry Daily*) and
      "Highlands Mission"
Poetry Northwest: "The Zero in the Branches"
Post Road: "Bones" and "Notebook"
Prairie Schooner: "Ditowagle," "War," and "Highlands Highway"
Smartish Pace: "Bird of Paradise"
The Virginia Quarterly Review: "Commission" (reprinted on
      Poetry Daily)

For my parents

Contents

Foreword

Mission Work is set in the Chimbu province of the central highlands of Papua New Guinea in the mid-1970s, more specifically, among a clan of the Kuman tribe known locally as the Paugokani, the clan Aaron Baker's family settles with and their missionary father "ministers" to. The memory time of the poems ranges, roughly, from Baker's sixth through his tenth year, a time parallel to the seminal period of Wordsworth's childhood years at the start of the two-part *Prelude*, though the learning emotion here is as anxious in its recollection as it is tranquil.

The themes that cross over Baker's remarkable sequence of poems represent preoccupations as much as perceptions: the tension between the values and rituals of a Western religion and those of the archetypes and myths of a "primitive" culture; the differences between peoples and kinds of families; and the separation from, yet collusion with, the past of a boy's primary years in an alien but compelling world. How do the assumptions of an abstract, invisible spiritual realm sort with those of an incarnate, relentlessly palpable, natural reality? Is the rain that fills the leaves of the great taban tree baptismal or merely restorative? Can it be the one and the other at the same time? Can the Bible sort with, let alone stand against, the bow and spear? ("I palm the black book. You notch your arrow.") Is it "white or black magic" that does the real mission work in the temple of the jungle? First came the gold seekers, then the coffee planters, to this isolated, rare native society — is the fieldwork of God any less exploitative?

Such themes and questions form much of the backstory of Baker's impressionistic, episodic self-revelations, in which his "Papuan" boyhood becomes both ordinary and extraordinary: on the one hand, he is home-schooled, befriended, pledged to fantasy and adventure; on the other hand, he is immersed in a totality of strangeness, actual danger, and the excitement of all manner of "blood debt." ("I came to a place where they killed a pig in my honor / and called me by something much like my name.") And running alongside the ongoing initiation rites projected in so many of the poems is Baker's relationship with and to his father, and his father's "business." ("Voices sing over the river where my bare-chested father / cradles the neck of a drenched boy lifted out of the water.") It is not so much that the speaker in the poems becomes any less devout, but that over the course of his experience with the Kuman he becomes exposed to and begins to absorb a larger, other consciousness. ("The farther mountains pulse with secret life — // we cup and taste their waters in our hands. / I felt the change I drank into myself.") Even Baker's father "has gone to the men's house. / Two days ago I saw him, golden beard and dusty khaki, / crouched with two men in the shade of a banana tree. / His eyes rose to watch me as I passed."

Yet the virtues of this exceptional first collection have only subversively to do with missionary themes and implicit cultural questions, religious and ethnic divides: Baker's is a book of acutely rendered backdrop landscape and wonderfully observed mise en scène, remembered as an adult through the pristine lens of childhood ("I am not a child as I lean into the memory / of a child's window, the jungle beyond it"), all of which heightens not only the poetry's sense of color and detail but its intuitive grasp of what is original in what is seen. In "Chimbu Wedding,"

> When the villagers stake out a hundred pigs
> and two men wade in with clubs,
> watch how they float, cold as light out of heaven,
> above the scene. When the pigs scream
> and buckle with their skulls caved in,
> remember that not one thing in this world
> will be spared.

In "Notebook,"

> Noon's light spread like an altar-cloth upon a field,
> the everywhere-glistening like birth of the inner forest,
>
> now everywhere I look is home.

Baker's gift for telescoping images is never simply visual or singular — it is always the double vision of his old world (Christianity) and his new world (Chimbu), melding. The "floating" men move as cold as light out of heaven; noon's light is an altar-cloth. This is perhaps the real subject of the subjectivity of the writing: the merging of Baker's childhood worlds with the merging of memory as an act of poetry. It is all done with such touch and flow of inevitability, with such animation, even animism:

> From air-fall to landfall, chapter and verse,
> I think of the spirit moving over the deep,
> the deep heaving to divide the waters.
> Of elsewhere entirely, my hereditary faith
> taking root in the difficult soil of Canaan.
> And only here and there a cast-out prophet
> in the sun-cracked wilderness dreaming of forests
> where the snake made his kingdom,
> mountains where no Adam walked
> and which no Adam named.

It is as if in reclaiming—actually, *discovering*—his Chimbu years, Baker claims a greater faith, or at least a faith of larger embrace: it is the artist in the poet whose mission it is to find—within our landscapes and separations and differences—unity, harmony, and reconciliation.

—Stanley Plumly

I

CHIMBU WEDDING

When the villagers stake out a hundred pigs
and two men wade in with clubs,
watch how they float, cold as light out of heaven,
above the scene. When the pigs scream
and buckle with their skulls caved in,
remember that not one thing in this world
will be spared. Not one leaf. Not one
hair on a child's head. See the women
hauling rocks to the fire-pits,
the boys kneeling to collect blood
in banana leaves, and think of St. Peter's
vision: cloven-hoofed creatures descending
on a sheet, the sky saying "Take, eat."
Learn to sit in the smoke with hunger sated
as children play with bladders they've inflated
like balloons. Learn a new language
for fellowship, and when you walk home
through the fields see if you can translate
the gloom-wrapped mountain's whisper
as *Come.* Then, if there is a place
prepared for the saints, you will know
which way to turn at the crossroads.
You will not trouble the angel at the garden
gate for a way past her sword. You will
not remember what blood washed you clean.

NOTEBOOK

Noon's light spread like an altar-cloth upon a field,
the everywhere-glistening like birth of the inner forest,

now everywhere I look is home.

Voices sing over the river where my bare-chested father
cradles the neck of a drenched boy lifted out of the water.

A brain of green fire, mountains roll
from the Chimbu in tightly ridged coils.

White boulders spilled upon the crests are places
to set my boots before I return on trails
through hilltop gardens   *Home.*

In my notebook I write letters to Grandma,
songs in pidgin, the names of plants from a textbook.

Jesus likem algeta, algeta, algeta.

Thanks for the books. I'm reading A Tale of Two Cities.
Next month I'll be twelve. Say hi to Grandpa.

Rhododendron, frangipani, dandelion, devil's claw.

    ▪ ▪ ▪

With my hand splayed before my face

I see in the spaces between fingers
smoke curl
          above roofs, pigs snuffle the dirt in their pens.

Black water glides between my knuckles,
black cliffs fall up from my fingertips

and village paths run into the world
　　like veins from both sides.

I make a fist because I can,
　　　　a little blood-light in the skin between bones.

How alike this is to prayer, that course
of brightness from the amber floorboards of my bedroom
that gathers in my folded hands

and coils to a substance behind closed eyes
before it knows how to rise.

I'd call this home,
forgetting the street of green squares in the States,
the two o'clock mail and six o'clock hiss of sprinklers

and take into my eye, Meugle, *though I was born on the other side
of the flood in old times and served other gods*

your skill with the hatchet,
the bravery that makes your dive sleek from the bridge,

Ditowagle, your quick laugh and cool center of patience,

so from my eye to my voice
I am not so strange, not so dangerous or different

from why you make a small ceremony of planting at the end
of the dry season or smear pig-grease on your skin when you marry.

　■　■　■

*Grandma, the drawing is of Weangle clouting the pig
that rooted up her sweet potatoes. Please give
this letter for Kevin to Mrs. Arnold.*

Myrmecodia, bamboo, pit-pit, banana.

This is how, though I needed for nothing
on the mountainside terrace and in the creek-bottomed canyon,

I came to a place where they killed a pig in my honor
and called me by something much like my name.

COMMISSION

Where memory divides like the first language

we kneel in the stained light of a chapel.
My father in a white shirt with rolled sleeves.
My mother's skirt gathered at her knees.

Anoint, Lord, their lips. The Holy Spirit speak
through each word and work of your servants —
this man — this woman — these two small boys —
as they labor in your fields.

From the subaqueous green at our backs,
the congregation is a warm breath that would raise us
as the minister moves between us for the laying on of hands.

When his palm moves from my shoulder
to my brother's, I close my eyes,

flex my fingers. Only my strength is in them.

■ ■ ■

Behind my grandmother's house,
light flares and dies in pastures above the evergreens.

This is the Northern silence, the smell of sap,
cold verticals and empty interiors.

The place before tree was *yaku bane* and rain *kamun,*
the place where memory would say it was from
when it left the tangled Papuan forests and wandered overseas.

■ ■ ■

With sixty native carriers, five gun-boys
watching the hillsides, the expedition

presses far into unmapped country.

Michael Leahy, camera and carbine slung on his shoulder,
considers the Wagai's terraced hillsides,
smoke curling above villages:

A *valley of perhaps twenty thousand souls.*

Gold-pans clatter as the column snakes through riverbeds
and along naked steeps. So far from their frontiers
there is no language here the interpreters will know.

It is not only necessary to establish communication
for trade and organizing labor, but to avoid hostilities.
Despite our guns, in this country it would be outright massacre.

Cries — like those of frightened birds — fly between hilltops.

■ ■ ■

Ni, father. *Na*, me.

Nina kata pagwa ene ditena ugwa:
        My father has come to tell you something.

Beyond the screened porch where I do math
our gardens spill down to the Ghanigai.

I draw straight lines along the ruler-edge
between points A and B

and pretend not to notice children watching
from the bamboo grove beside the garden.

My father has gone to the men's house.
Two days ago I saw him, golden beard and dusty khaki,
crouched with two men in the shade of a banana tree.
His eyes rose to watch me as I passed.

■ ■ ■

8

When I helped to nail boards for the new house
I learned that *edi* was the word for both wood and truth

in the way *kobuglo* meant both money and stone
and *kuri* both sister and star.

My mother and brother fingered in bulbs,

strung the lines now dangling with green tomatoes.
I runneled the ditches,
a dull orange of hacked clay between plots.
Each evening I draw from a rain barrel to water the roots.

Where the slope falls at the garden's edge,
high kunai grass, white stones at the river,

the water still and black.

■ ■ ■

When one large kina shell could buy a month's labor,
the Leahys hired a hundred natives to build
the first airstrip in Hagen. When the brush
had been burned, the ground raked, the workers locked
elbows and danced to flatten the earth.

We think that good things are coming out of the sky,
mothers told their children,
and the dance was to bring the good things down.

Massa Mick said that in three days a ballus — *a big bird —*
would come. And when it did come, dipping down it made a big noise.
Some ran and hid. Some lay covering their heads
and shit themselves in fear and confusion.

A boy of ten was chosen to fly to the coast so he could
return and tell what he saw. *Do not eat their food*
or you will go mad, his mother told him.

He saw white buildings, the sea, and boats at anchor.
He took food when it was given and ate thinking
Now I will go mad.

He asked for a bottle to carry some of the sea.
He saw a horse, thought it a massive pig,
and laughed to see a man carried on its back.
He asked for a cutting of its tail.

Returning home, he told what he'd seen.
The people didn't believe, so he gave them the bottle,
which they passed, gravely tasting the sea.

They touched the tuft of horsehair, and the boy's
uncle wound it around a stick for a totem of healing.

      ■ ■ ■

I lose sight of the gardens,
climb barefoot from the frustrated order of forest paths.

Cloud forest. Mosquito-buzz,
papery flight of cicadas,
pollen swimming through sunlight.

I do not know where my father is.

Tall stalks of wild ginger, myrmecodia covered with ants.

Rising into the clouds and returning
from where his father and mother will never go,
the boy's face must be touched by his mother
before she will believe he is alive.

Only after his father looks hard in his eyes, can he speak.

      ■ ■ ■

ade bemara
place where the sun sets
ade umara
place where the sun rises

I still want the words to say
I have come among you to be saved

to pass between you like food and drink,
to live inside you and be nourished,
to love as God is said to love from the other side of silence.

I have been told that what must
be redeemed has been redeemed,
that love is the unspoken as well as the spoken syllable,

that I need only take heaven into the eye,
love the scabbed knees of the elect,
the palsied spear-hand of the elder.

But for my tongue, tangled as if in gauze,

aga gogl ki,
to be ashamed.

They say there are lost spirits that wander the forest
and may not reenter the fold

though a greater spirit waits in our blood and on our lips
to fuse our fouled scattered tongues

into a tongue of fire that leaps over the land.

How would it be to wander the land and be lost?
What memory would I try to pass back to the living?

What love reach through me,
like a worm through speech, for the world?

CARGO CULT

See how this works: I'm a dead boy come over the water.

Skin pale since it's bloodless, hair bleached blond

by the sun of an unforested country, I bring good

blades and fine cloth. My voice is strange music

and I want nothing of yours. There's health

in my touch. *Eat the bread, drink the blood*

and the sea, which for so long delivered only

upcoast coconuts, handfuls of shells

for charms, and scraps of meat that lay in the froth

to be picked at by gulls, will now cast up God.

BONES

We did not know why the spirits of our dead
returned until we saw them wade into the river
and sift sand and rocks for their bones.

Yes, I was young and ignorant,
full of the superstitions of my people.

Once I stole a pig from my brother-in-law.
Once I cut hair from a sleeping girl
and worked magic so she would lie with me,

and there was the time working the gold-fields
I stole a knife from one of the boys
Massa Mick brought over the mountains.

Yes, I was a bad and worthless man,
but now I will rise up from the dead.

■ ■ ■

Now I will rise up from the dead.
Now I will rise up from the dead, enter heaven,

though without my brother and parents
who went into the ground before the new time.

I will cry for them and my sister with me,
Jesus wipe the tears from our eyes.
I will rise up from the dead

but not go into the earth to look for my lands.

I will sing of the blood that flows into my new body
and not return to look for my bones.

My soul is the secret of labor.
A dredge on the river won't find it.

The cross on the hill — can it notice? — or dial
on the coffee scale measure?

My soul is what's missing for heaven.
Only I know where I have hid it.
My people are all dead or dying.

God gives me the strength of without-them.

I am alone on a hill facing Jesus, who twists on a tree
since he needs me. I want to be kind to all people.

I am alone in the village, I miss you. The time
for deciding is over. Yes, this is my time of rejoicing.

While I'm waiting in heaven, I'll enter
the river and lie there
                    in pieces you'll never find later,

when you look, since you have to, from wanting
to rise from your life into heaven.

BLOOD DEBT

The spirits of ancestors are uneasy. When wasn't this true?
And who remembers more about the blood debt

than that it is unpaid, so long and always unpaid?

Noon: man-high shields line the men's house
as warriors sharpen arrows in the shade.

Nightfall: a dance in full feathers in the glare of the flames.

Dawn: the procession begins, steady rhythm of drums —
clatter of spears, bows and arrows and shields.

Silence: the enemy, one mountain over, waits massed on a field.

BIRD OF PARADISE

In the half-light behind the chapel,
my father takes my head in his hands.

      "See it?" he whispers
and twists my head like picking a delicate fruit.

    Inside at the altar Ditowagle strums
a three-chord progression, pauses, repeats
        as I search the foliage —

light-speckled mass of branches and leaves —
         for the golden outline
  I have seen on the flag of this country,

and try to imagine how it must look
      perched there, tail trailing behind it,
so near to me,
           a gift of the rarest of birds.

Still, I cannot untangle it from darkness
      and the music, faltering,
falls to where it must begin
  again, from an almost impossible distance,

a music of swamp-light;
      of an eye
imparted sight by a hand passed
      between it and the world like a wing.

What difference to the eye that sees far
    enough in if there was never a bird,
if the bird has already flown?

THE TABAN TREE

from a Misinmin children's story

The moon's water was sweet.
It streamed from your netbag in the hut.
I cupped a little in my hands and drank
while you worked in the garden.

And where has the moon gone
that I kept to bury with your father?

When I unwrapped it, it rolled
through the ashes on the floor.
It climbed up the taban tree and into the sky.
Think, Mother, how small beads of water
will lie on the grass blades at morning.

But where has my son gone,
you with eyes that shine like stones
underwater? Yes, I have seen
how moss glows on the taban
where the moon left its mark.

SECOND GENESIS

Bees float in the frangipanis behind the chapel.
The day's wash hangs limp on the line.

Meugle's father has gone to battle,
mine to set the Bible against the bow and spear.

We train a telescope on the hills.
Women move slowly through the fields.

I see, says Meugle, *the Dagle Mitna sitting on their shields,*
my father and Apa drawing arrows in the brush.

I lean in for a look, see in the circle of light
a woman bowed over her garden.

Yes, I say, *your father has killed a man.*

Meugle nods, his thoughts more distant from me
than our fathers. I see beside the woman
a naked child weaving garlands out of grass.

■ ■ ■

Will you find me where I'm hid?
Have angels finished wrestling in these fields?

Our battle is not against flesh and blood —

I palm the black book. You notch your arrow.
Our fathers are at war with our brothers.

We'll be a single son of this country
when each has killed half of the other.

■ ■ ■

Flight through the rain-streaked half-light,
thick splatter on fronds.

The pig crashes through the underbrush,
frayed rope snaking after him.

I snort, slip in the mud, scramble head-first
through brambles and vines,

then rise in the clearing
where Meugle lifts the pig,
snout gripped shut by a fist.

Pulsing at my throat, my life.
Meugle kneels to use the knife.

  ■ ■ ■

In the game of war, our spears are stalks of fern.

I lie in the hillside grass and take my turn
as a sleeping sentry. Even in play, I feel a sudden fear

of his dark shape on the sky. When he strikes,
I writhe and die around my wound.

He shouts, raises his spear. When I rise,
he wipes grass seeds from my shoulders and hair.

  ■ ■ ■

Smells of woodsmoke and sweat fill the cool of the hut.
Meugle's wet face glows over the fire.
He rolls a sweet potato from the embers with a stick,

touches my shin with its still-warm tip — *Ene Yegwa,* yours.
I hold the potato in both hands, decide it's my heart,

that I will keep it hot as long as I can.

He frowns, touches me again with the stick.
I peel the black skin from the soft white meat.
When Meugle smiles, my throat gluts with thanks.

  ■ ■ ■

He kneels and fingers my welts,
says that evil sorcery brought up the bees.

He covers me with deep handfuls of mud from the river.
                Good sorcery, he says,
and as the mud dries, it draws out the sting.

But he keeps adding more. His fingers
move over me, fashion a helmet for my skull,
broaden my chest and shoulders

until I whirl away,
flinging mud and splashing up water.

Meugle crouches,
amazed at the work of his hands

as the mudman dances, impervious to pain —

and I can't tell if this is white or black magic,
his gestures to summon or ward me away.

SING-SING KIAMA

This landscape a music
    of severe undulations
        river gorges, limestone cliffs,

mist-dissolved mountains
    The tree snake's skin dried
        and stretched over a drum.

Scope and perspective —
    a problem of where to place
        feet in the dance.

Flex fingers back
    so only palms slap the drum.
        Three shuffles in the dust,

four beats. Four beats and a turn.
    The dark takes the forest,
        dips into the valleys,

the dark takes the rivers. Woodsmoke.
    Beads shake. Face-paint
        in firelight. Four turns

and a leap. Palms sting on snake-
    skin. The sky turning black.
        The ground leaping up,

the dark drumming back.

SPIRITS OF THE LOW GROUND

The knives are calling
out for their fathers,

the skinning knife
and the warrior's, the knife
of the mother in the kau-kau field,

the knife the murderer hid under a stone.

The dead will not lean in
from the mountains
a millennium longer, their hands

out, their mouths pursed with want.

I have known since my birth
they would come,
drifting like smoke up the river,

spitting blood and shedding
their snakeskins at nightfall.

Tonight I will burn my hut, scatter
my name in its ashes —

I have heard the knife I lost
as a boy in the forest

start to sing in its sleep.

THE RED SNAKE

Something about memory: the story of Daniel
        in my brother's illustrated reader,
the charcoal-colored angel raising her fingers

        to a lion's lip. And something about
forgetfulness: clouds pouring over the mountains,
        coffee-leaves flashing their pale undersides.

On the covered porch, he spells out words,
        lips twisting with this new problem
of letters. With my book closed,
        I'm watching him. *A story of brothers.*

        ■ ■ ■

When I became a man, I put away all childish things . . .

        But when he was six, under the single bulb
in our grandmother's basement, he wrapped his baseball glove
        in shirts that won't fit him again

and put it away in a cardboard box labeled SIMON.

        I see him in the glare off the river, as shoulders
sloped under a netbag of lemons, he and another
        walk into our ambush of dirt clods.
Two brothers went into the field

        Iambagle screams and flees upriver as Meugle
and I lift Simon — arms and legs — and pitch him
        into the water. Afterward,

we all sit together and suck on the lemons.
        We kill, are killed, so often in these games.

        ■ ■ ■

The worst thing, it's whispered, is to go into the ground,
        to go into the ground, take pieces of flesh
from a man killed in battle and fly over the hills

        to the enemy to give the bits to their sorcerer —
magic against your own people. Finding you out,

your true brothers will cut out your tongue,
        bind and burn you on your hut unless
you tell them that while you slept in the forest,

        a red snake found you and crawled down your throat.
That the snake lives in your stomach
        and you are asleep while he acts.

That you are asleep when you go into the ground.

        ▪ ▪ ▪

Gravely, he sets the steaming bowls around —
        each dollop of overboiled potatoes
and carrots topped with a sprig of fresh parsley.

This is to be a meal from his hands,
        and he has refused a chicken from Ditowagle
because it was not from his garden.

        He sits upright before his bowl until
we all have tasted. Our father swallows a spoonful
        of this flavorless pap, calls it good.

        ▪ ▪ ▪

My brother: drinker of Orange Fanta, drooler
        of ripe tomatoes. Giver of gifts.
Early riser. Easy to tears. Slow learner of language.
        My brother, player of the ukulele.
Rider of a bicycle too large for his body.
        Poor runner. Strong swimmer.

A brother will not travel by daylight over enemy fields
        but come by night to the place where he failed you,
giving ground or running from ambush.

        He will have roped shut a pig's snout,
and when the blade slits
        its throat and the pig's blood is poured

into yours, rise and fill its shuddering flesh
        with your life. Nestle there

under your brother's arm. Share his heart's throb
        to the race through the dark, and returning
among your mother and sisters, do not scorn their weeping.

        Forget, as they swallow the meat
piece by piece, how enemy shields
        drew close and drowned out the light.

Forget. Fill their mouths with remembering.
        Withdraw, gentle brother, your curse on the living.

Come again in the health of the ground and the rains.

BRIDE PRICE

My mother taught me which leaf to chew for tooth-pain,
    the feather for fortune,
but finally laid me down

amidst a vast ceremony of smoke

where, as from the forest's lost patience,
    a creature began whispering
over the speeches one world over of fathers.

        Bamboo poles
fluttering with bills dip, changing hands.

I am gone out from the land of my people
      and through voices bled as by distance,

the dark of the mountains floats down
    into the shape that commands me.
Blackened with pig-grease and ash,

wearing a headdress of white egret,
    whose body drifts there at the edge of the dance
if not the slow shadow of death
      or a husband?

THE WEAVER

Knuckles bulge above thumbtips weaving
bamboo-strips, a little flush of white on dented
skin, a little rasp of friction on the wood.
Blades of kunai shaken free of dirt
are wound around the slats to hold them fast.
Somewhere in the corner of one eye,
a locust stirs within a mound of chaff,
and farther back, within the sunlight's swirl
of dust, a shape begins to cheat toward
the substance of the hand. Scattered shavings
and the smell of pitch, the knife's glint against
the dullness of a stone, dissolve before the vision
of a house. The weaver stands to stretch in a new place.
A pattern — *home* — lies flat amidst the waste.

THE ZERO IN THE BRANCHES

Between wars, the old wars brood over our bodies.
Stunned — having once fed so well —
they drift toward sleep as they starve.

Look: high in the canopy, forty years
since it fell almost to earth, the fuselage
hangs, its Rising Sun a circle of rust.

Vines spill like a Gorgon's hair
from the cockpit,
birds nest in the guns,

and from the wings, tree spiders spin
sunlight out of hatred from heaven.
May it never reach earth. May it hang there

forever so we can come, as often as needed,
to let its strange peace come over us
when we think of the skeleton slumped

in a moldering uniform over the shattered
yoke, the tree-snakes pouring over the jaw
like an unsilenceable, unlistened-to tongue.

HOW DO YOU LIKE YOUR BLUE-EYED BOY?

Water-swirl, sky-swirl,
     light splaying over the grass. Let heaven
happen without me. Burnt clouds

     uncoil into the blue — no messages there —
while downriver gunmen advance forty years earlier,
     faces blotted out beneath hat-brims.

No one's left to sound the alarm. But let them
     come, let them happen without me.
 In the illustrated *Huckleberry Finn*

     torn from a brown-paper package
three months from America, I looked a long while
     at one picture: a darkly penciled

 dirt road beside a river, a lightly penciled silhouette
of a barefoot boy in a cocked straw hat
strolling into the scribbles. So let the birds

     come, the words come and the worms,
and don't cry when I return for my funeral
     after a little sleep, a little folding of the hands —

II

DEPARTURES

The redeemer comes a dark way.
— THEODORE ROETHKE

Vague murmurings from a distant coast:
the mountain road trails off like an unfinishable sentence.
History arrives, recedes in the airplane's

faraway drone. A 9-volt radio blares the national anthem
inside a hut, a jeep's dust-plume blossoms
on the hillcrest.
                              How much easier it would be

to rise to the level of the treetops, watch men stack
sacks of coffee in the village square,
women haul their daily kau-kau from the fields,

than it is to grow into a body among them.

At journey's end, the road deeper in starts
          in my eye — *No, back,*
farther back —

          ▪ ▪ ▪

Swedish missionaries Bergman and Eliere
gazed like Moses from their accidental summit

at woodsmoke curled like hundreds of question marks
over green grids and cut terraces.
They swore themselves to silence, but brothers,

we have found out your secret of village-crammed
canyons. Of *gold, gold,* and souls for the salvaging.
Your Divine Commission —
                              did you forget
or remember it? — when you sneaked with clenched
jaws out of history and into the Edie Creek
fields, where prospectors hot from Australia
strained their claims in the still
narrow coast-bound margin of Mandated Territory.

          ▪ ▪ ▪

Jul 8: Ewunga creek. Traces show moderately
well for dredging propositions though at £4 ounce
little offerings for the individual claim.
Park-like sing sing areas & homesteads
surrounded by ornamental shrubs. Plenty
standing timber & grass would make
boyhouse building easy, & good possibilities
for hydroelectric power schemes if there were
anything improved. I can already picture about
four dredges tearing up the flats lower down.
Human bones on the banks & showing in our
pans says BIG population farther up. Local kanakas
very excited about our stopping & brought
plenty of kai. Taylor, nervous, fires over
their heads to keep them a comfortable distance.

■ ■ ■

Is this the way we set against the heart,
provisions scant, our maps absurdly wrong?

The farther mountains pulse with secret life —

we cup and taste their waters in our hands.
I felt the change I drank into myself.
Each door I passed was to my father's house.

Drawn on by deeper greens and giddier
precipices, I became this version of the land's.
            Good news! Good news!
I am your happy son. My classmates smile

from a photo on my shelf. Still, we strike
our camps and press always
farther on. Will the inhabitants greet us?

Will we know wealth from mortal hazard,
the highland home from the mountain too far,
our own country well enough to ever return?

■ ■ ■

I know which floorboard it's under —
black book like a Bible that opens
on rows of yellow vials.
                    Secret substance,
last resort. Like that time they brought

the charred baby, its raised hands trembling
from the table where we'd just eaten breakfast
and we couldn't remember — wet or dry compresses?

My brother was there, pale-faced for a while,
before he drifted away, taking all our thoughts
with him. Out came the needle, one last bite
of goodbye. "You have to watch them all the time,"

my mother kept saying. Which of the weeping
women was the mother? My father —
        efficient, taut-faced, mercy —
was the one pushing the plunger.

        ∎ ∎ ∎

Brothers, make peace with him.
This is the white-skinned giant Souw,
who went from the land out of shame
when he was found with his daughter.
He knows which trees hold up the sky
and will cut them down for his tent-poles.
He will release his dogs, starved in the world
of the dead, on the living. Men fall
with each crack of shield-splintering lightning —
do not go against him again with your spears.
Take your daughters, adorned as for marriage,
and walk with downcast eyes. Bring pigs,
gourds of water. Bring wood for his fires.
Do not speak to remind him of his disgrace
and if he strikes, do not raise your hand.

        ∎ ∎ ∎

Said Aaron, "Do not be angry at me.
You know how wicked the people are.
I threw gold in the fire. Out came
this bull-calf and the people worshipped it."

But just a little gold, just a little spark from the dust,
the cassowary's claw, bat-bones, necklaces
of kina and seed.
                    Bird of paradise plumes.
The long motion of the Ghanigai River.

Red betel-nut juice and pig-shit. Peach-fuzz
on my cheek and under my arms. Sounds
of rustling leaves, thin notes on bamboo flutes.
Smells of kerosene, woodsmoke, the pith
of vines, of pitch on arrow-tips and drum-skins.

My name, *Aaron*, on a young woman's tongue.
In the fire at midnight, my voice can't crack
a prayer to any god in the flames.

        ▪ ▪ ▪

Something skids from the tree's crotch
with a sound like skin on skin.
A winged queen burrows into the muck.

The fronds start to waver. My arms
have grown golden. I think like a son.
I'm rippling out in my reflection on water.

In the corner of my eye, a king swims to earth
in the sun's swirl of pollen. Creation has

fallen. My ankles rock into the mud
as I crouch. My hands can't be hidden.
Veins rise into the angles of my wrists.

        ▪ ▪ ▪

Jungle-shrouded secret
of a garden.
Ring of stakes
hammered into the ground.
Who thought they could keep me from this tree,

slick-skinned fruit
that fits my hand like a heart?
Loving its weight, purple gloss in the light,
I push in the knife
point first and scoop

the pulp into my mouth.
I stick out my sweetened tongue
                    see world, see . . .
and leave the skin on a spike
where its keeper will find it.

     ■ ■ ■

Kumanka na kiurika,
                    I don't understand Kuman.
The jungle rolling over and away,
limestone cliffs and mist-covered mountains.
Yes, Kuman is difficult,

            Owo Kumanka yombuglo orukwa.
Naked children giggle to touch my pale skin,
to run fingers through my yellow hair.
Ene "friend" kaioko siragle wedtime?
            How do you say "my friend" in the language?

Iniga, says Meugle, a boy of my height
with a deep ragged scar from his throat to his ear.

     ■ ■ ■

Everywhere, false lights frame mornings
that never were,
                    where we are happy
and in possession of our powers, where natives
crowd riverbanks singing salvation and throng

as one body to the cross and coffee plantation alike.
Was there ever a country to live in but this one?

Pharisees beat their breasts at the temple —
they have had their reward.
                          We too, we bitter,
unlovely lice-ridden liars with scabies
scabbed over, are proud when we name

our transgressions. And then what?
Our righteousness like filthy rags — hold that thought.

Our eyes know what they've seen.
Our bodies bow to their work as they can.

TARO

1

Cold and stinking of viscera
     the mist coiled on the path between huts.

Snake heads roiled amidst faces
     of hollow-eyed spirits — a thousand mouths
  hissing a man-killing word.

Those who heard sighed and lay down
     without speaking,
  eyes rolled to the sun, and then starved —

and so people, the only ones
     then in the world, fled to the mountains
  and lived unclothed like animals,
digging grubs from the ground

2

until a brother and sister sneaked back to the village.
     They put clay in their ears —
  still they heard a woman's voice

sing from the trees: *Children, where are you? Come —*
     your mother is hungry.
  "Don't cry," said the sister

through a grumble like sickness in a dying man's chest.
     "Big sister, I'm here," gasped
  the brother and the earth split

with the bad breath and moist hiss of over-roasted skin.
     A white worm writhed out
  of the dirt, and when it grasped

his sister's foot, the boy began swinging both hatchets.
      Glints against blackness
   like a caught moth beating its wings.

3

When the children were found the next morning,
      they woke and were grateful for water.
   Answering none of the too many

questions, they planted the hacked-up worm's pieces,
      and leaves soon grew out
   of the ground. This is the story

told even by children of how people found food and were saved.
      The word is made flesh. Learn to eat it.
   We've survived on what grew from a grave.

READ AND SAY NOTHING

What I want most — what I wish —

No. The facts — let's begin there.

My mother said "Sit. Read and say nothing."
Yes, that was it. "Sit. Read and say nothing"
and went on kneading the wash until the men
came into the yard. She smiled —
she's smiling, raising one sud-soaked hand
from the basin and he — the captain nodded —
I mean, now he is nodding —
moving his hand from his holster
and I'm reading —

What are you reading?

No. I am not reading.
The breeze lifts one edge of her skirt —

and the dozen or so policemen —
I think there must be a dozen or more —
are eyeing our pineapples and tomatoes.
I look at one word without reading
and now they are stomping downriver
in their black boots and she is plunging
her hands in the water as if to wash clean her lie.

She is what?

I'm sorry. She is washing her hands.

ALBINO

Left behind in the dark,
   secret son,
your bawling startles the sunlight
   on the branches
crowding the path from the garden.

Can you know why
   she lays you aside?
Why my footsteps hesitate
   and pass by?
Broken off from her sleeping

the day is a swelter
   of silence
you squirm through
   as the dark beneath the thatch
takes weight
   from the afternoon sun.

But if sometimes,
   little brother,
the dark is the best skin
   we'll have —
I've been told enough times
   to believe it —
in the end all of us burn.

A PRAYER

My father, deep in malarial fever, keeps floating away
on his bed.
          Damp rag in my fist. Knot in my neck.
Night beyond the curtains is gathering silence.
My father's slick face twists, as if in deep concentration
on a single idea.
              Sick light of a lantern, stink of vomit and sweat.
My mother keeps putting her hands on my shoulders.
        My father sits up, I hand him the bucket.
When he's done with it, I give him water.
        "Put your hands on me," he asks, so we do it.
My mother folds her hands in his. Mine go palm-down
        on his chest.
             Deep breaths in the stillness.
He flutters his eyelids.
            I intone, as he's taught me,
a request for God's mercy if it's His will to give it,
for His strength if it's not.
           My father's whole body trembles.
His life rises again and again in my hands.

ABOVE KEROWAGI

Black and yellow lichen-spotted limestone,
mosquito-loud shadows full of cold-kept secrets,

the smell of copper in stagnant red pools.
Rivulets spume from underground,

slide in slick diffusion down the rock face
where I make out grimaces of stone,

moss beards flapping, tongues of froth.
Who dragged corpses to the cave,

loose heels knocking up the path,
hands trailing as if to find some futile

hold on the world? No one knows or will say.
Above the cave-mouth, switchbacks

dissolve into the lemon light. Meugle
takes my rucksack, taps a smoke

as I crouch through the blood-scented
black toward a distant *drip drip* of water.

Boots crunch tinder-bones of fingers and feet
as I raise my trembling beam to the web-

shrouded orgy of the heaps:
fused pelvises and rib cages, jutting fibulas,

toothless skulls lolling away from the light
to face down the cave's off-kilter throat

where, if anything comes for them now,
it will come. I stiffen my spine as with insult,

steady the beam into every corner
of the cave, and know with first urgency

that God will come into this world from the bit
of blue that remains. He will come

and I will leave with my skin. Faces nod
in my light, keep their distance and grin.

WAR

My mother — smell of lavender —
moves in the dark hallway between her empty bed
　　　and where we sit cross-legged with comic books

in one lantern's circle of light.

Somnambulant warriors move —
　　　　　a wave through the grass —
　　in the permanent elsewhere of fathers.

Goodnight boys, don't forget prayers
　　　　as inside me the man — secret body, secret skill —
　　　　　　closes his comics and draws his bowstring

ignoring the voice on the hilltop
bursting with correct finally-found fury
　　　from the ambulance-jeep's gentle purr —

Lay it down! Lay it down! Love your brother!

But I've glimpsed my enemy, mischievous twin,
　　　dancing between tree-trunks,

　heard the signal clatter of spears against shields,
felt strength lengthen my muscles and tighten
　　to a tension that can no longer be kept —

There you are　　there you are

the love I've created flies for your heart.

EVIL SPIRIT

*When the Leahy brothers came into the Chimbu, we thought they
were the ghosts of our ancestors. Their carriers chewed betel-nut
and we believed their red spit was the blood of their victims.*

—A PAUGOKANI TRIBESMAN

Their coming stirred me from my sleep in the treetops.

I breathed the rich smell of swamp-rot,
watched leaves overcrawling with insects,

a tree-snake's uncoiling,
an eyeless pink rat in her nest amidst roots.

I circled the villages like a hungry dog.

The ghosts raised a house high on Gumani imbu
and when I saw that it burned all night

but stood whole in the morning, I decided.
I lay down for six days in the swamp.

Mud held my hand as worms moved
to remake me. Water pooled
in my eye-sockets and a bird of paradise

crawled between my ribs for a heart.
The forest fell silent when I rose.

I tested my hands on each other.

I could not hold the world still with my vision.
My feet found a path through the forest.

I came to that house and I entered.
I spoke the words expected

of a loving, a long-returning son.

IN GURU WOODS

What shape did you glimpse,
traced by light-laced branches
in the thicket's heart? A man's?

Was it just a trick of the eye?
Something conjured of the hidden
marsupial's fear, the noise of water
over the sand-bottomed creek?

Did a spirit watch at the edge
of its sight as you passed
along one path of its world?

There are so many roads into this forest,
but you can leave by just one.

Already, you are disappearing
amidst light motes, smells of pollen.

Already, you cannot remember
what you sought here, so far from home.

DARKNESS LEGEND

*After accounts of "the time of darkness," when fallout from
a coastal volcano blanketed the Highlands for several days in
the late eighteenth or early nineteenth century*

Through the sunless three days' scour of ash, many who could not sleep
or take food through mud-clotted throats survived by madness,
drinking it like water. This is how we learned that the field's brightness
is the gleam in the open eye of a sleeping lunatic, that the cane's sweetness

and the smell of frangipanis teach the tongue sulfur and suffocation
sits in the feel of sunlight on skin. Listen, through the dog's whimper,
through stones from the sky pattering on the village path, listen in the silences
between laughter of those who laugh with the land for your *place of peace*

and still water. Do you see how girls smile at these stories of old men?
How even the weakest man walks proudly past the meeting places
of the strong? I tell you that this is how it was with the old tribe
before even the most ignorant learned what place a man has in this world.

The Big Man — do any remember a time when he didn't haul sacks of coffee
from one place to another? — when he didn't ride in a Toyota for being
the greatest flatterer? He lives a short time and then takes up his death
like a well-balanced spear. He is rightly honored by a cutting off of fingers

but in a time of darkness, he is of less use than the sucking infant
and goes over first, blood-in-the-mouth. Then he is more dangerous
to his children than the starved spirits that belch from the ground and roam
the villages in the shapes of men. Then even the cleverest sorcerer,

burning his hair, dipping totems in ash stirred with spit, is shown
by smoke-in-his-eye the village's same smothered square, the same bamboo
walls and thatch roofs roaring like men and whimpering like women.
You've heard it said that because our bodies were not formed of the soil

like the cassowary and opossum we must not wake the woods with loud
or unruly talk. But why not take the ax to the sacred trees? Why not
put on white shirts and sing with white men? Truly, says the preacher,
it's best to forget this world and ask the next one into your heart.

DITOWAGLE

Dark lowers like a hand over the kau-kau fields
    as she crosses them.
A figure slighting side to side,
    a shape diminishing to one spot on a purpling tableau.

Dishes washed, water basin filled and set out
    for morning, she goes.
She goes and tomorrow

    I wear the shirt creased by her hands.
I'll remember the river,
    her body turned on the bank with loose,
almost demure surrender,

    the river, but also how she crawled
with us between the garden rows
    plucking weeds with her quick nine fingers.
Between her knees, so she could run

    her fingers through my sun-scorched hair,
I'd feel the child stirring there.
    Father to the fatherless:
that child drowned within her drowning.

    Now drawn to disappearance down
the aperture of herself, the forest
    takes her and I watch an empty field

for one never limned in twilight,
    for a soul, or what we know of it—
a light around a body that can darken and be lost.

THE DAY AND THE HOUR

If he appeared on the border with the enemy,
        appeared and came slowly like a sleepwalker
through the grass, the news would fly between villages.

        He fell from the sky in his white sheet and blond
beard. No, the ground shook and he rose from the river.
        I heard the Dagle Mitna sing of this in their gardens.

If he came carrying no gold-pans or books, came armed
        with neither rifle nor spear. *He has come*
to destroy us and to stay in these lands where he lived

        before there were people. No — his looks are kind.
He has come to love us and take away pain. If we saw him
        a long way off, a knife's swath through the kunai,

my father would kneel to wait, my mother not leave
        his side but call for us to hide. Under the bed,
my brother's breath hot at my neck, we would stifle

        our cries even when we heard the floorboards
creak, the rustle, the blaze, when he drew back the sheet.
        When one of us gasped, we wouldn't know which,

and the rest white light, the faraway noise of voices
        half-remembered, the rest being carried to sleep as a child.

THE LAST WAY

A way to begin: my brother's breaths steady and deepen,
a dead lantern's whiff of kerosene, curtains stirring
to insinuate the windowsill

in the orange room

              where I am nine and first feeling
the whole world strain its darkness to make vivid
a procession of torches at the riverbank.

On the bamboo mat the corpse
shines against the river
with the light it has waited a whole lifetime for.

The second way: I am not a child as I lean into the memory
of a child's window, the jungle beyond it,
lean that first time over the dark bookshelf,

its set of *Grolier's Children's Encyclopedia,*
stacked comic books, and illustrated Bible
        where nothing is written about evil spirits

that enter and animate the dead
if not warded off for two nights with music and fire,
about craven acts, perversities
                to be performed until
the fly-bitten corpse collapses in the tropical noon.

Flute-song rises, thin as wind between stars,
falls until there's no sound but the torches' flickering

and I am left with the last way:

a spirit that longs toward
        the shapes of those it remembers,

wanting only to say "Hear me. I have been misunderstood,"

before stillness falls over it
            and fire bears it on.

HIGHLANDS HIGHWAY

Through the cold predawn and dew-drenched
    silence of the last day, villagers drift
out of the coffee trees to throng around

    the idling jeep piled high with roped-together
crates. Bodies move through the downcast
    beams, exhaust roiling around them —
this is not the dream I have in which

I am always arriving, a bright afternoon
    on the first day of an epoch. That the faces
I learned — Kondilwagie, Apa, Meugle —

should blend together like vapors —
    what use will I have for attention again?
Goodbye, goodbye, as I walk a last time

    through my boyhood, kiss cheeks
and press bodies. *Goodbye, goodbye —*
    already the house filtering toward
invisibility in first light through the trees.

HIGHLANDS MISSION

1

Mists open like wings over childhood's island,
green folds riding over the Pacific,
valleys overbrimming with beech, pandanus, casuarina,
jungle specked red and orange with untasted fruit.

From air-fall to landfall, chapter and verse,
I think of the spirit moving over the deep,
the deep heaving to divide the waters.
Of elsewhere entirely, my hereditary faith
taking root in the difficult soil of Canaan.
And only here and there a cast-out prophet
in the sun-cracked wilderness dreaming of forests
where the snake made his kingdom,
mountains where no Adam walked
and which no Adam named.

2

Parrots and cockatoos, hawks, swiftlets,
birds of paradise, flutter in and out of shadows.

The first mammals, Melanesian swine, swam ashore
bringing unclean spirits from the country where they were driven,
by a word, from the mountains into the sea.

They waited along their paths for Nopu,
father of the tribes, to enter the Highlands with his bow,
bamboo knife, and stone adze.

Nopu's dog was their enemy and they hated,
from hiding, the bright circle of men at their fire.

3

Who can say where such spirits will settle
in their long migrations through roots and raindrops,
whose tongues they will touch, whose hearts?

The land lies like the body of a sleeping lord,

giving and withholding its favors.
Tossing restlessly, burying whole villages in mud.

I sat with an old woman who gave me a roasted
sweet potato at the edge of her garden.
Having no common language, we chewed
with the abstracted thoughtfulness of those Corinthians
at communion whom St. Paul addressed saying

For he that eateth and drinketh unworthily
eateth and drinketh damnation to himself,
not discerning the Lord's body.

4

News came from Mount Hagen of two missionaries
dragged from their jeep and hacked to death with machetes.

At night, the old sorcerer came down from the hill
and walked through the forest with a flaming stick.

"It is good magic," assured our house-girl Ditowagle.
"It silences spirits."
"Perhaps she's right," said my father.

He returned to his study, leaned over a lantern.

5

Creation, we tell ourselves, looking to the lip
of the mountains, the rain's slant across fields.

At what place should we enter it? The river's long
motion, the bats flying, accurate in their hunger,
through the deep-forest whine of mosquitoes.

At what places have we entered already?

Shadows shift through the rows of coffee trees at the yard edge.
The sorcerer's brand burns beneath the cross on the hill.

Notes

"Commission" and "Departures" incorporate events and quotations drawn from the letters and journals of members of the Leahy brothers' 1933 expedition into the interior highlands of Papua New Guinea. The source for this material is Bob Connolly and Robin Anderson's *First Contact* (Penguin, 1997).

"Sing-sing Kiama" is based on a traditional dance of the Bundi people, which is described in detail in David G. Fitz-Patrick and John Kimbuna's book *Bundi* (Ryebuck, 1983).

"Highlands Mission" owes a debt to Peter Matthiessen's *Under the Mountain Wall* (Viking, 1962), specifically for its story of Nopu, the father of the tribes.

Acknowledgments

I'd like to thank the Virginia Center for the Creative Arts, the Ludwig Vogelstein Foundation, the Bread Loaf Writers' Conference, and the students and faculty of the creative writing programs at the University of Virginia and Stanford University. Additionally, I want to thank the following individuals for their indispensable advice and support during the completion of this book: Gaby Calvocoressi, Michael Collier, Sarah Gambito, Joseph Legaspi, Thorpe Moeckel, Stanley Plumly, Joseph Powell, and Sean Singer.

And above all, thanks to Jennifer Chang.

Bread Loaf and the Bakeless Prizes

The Katharine Bakeless Nason Literary Publication Prizes were established in 1995 to expand the Bread Loaf Writers' Conference's commitment to the support of emerging writers. Endowed by the LZ Francis Foundation, the prizes commemorate Middlebury College patron Katharine Bakeless Nason and launch the publication career of a poet, a fiction writer, and a creative nonfiction writer annually. Winning manuscripts are chosen in an open national competition by a distinguished judge in each genre. Winners are published by Houghton Mifflin Company in Mariner paperback original.

2007 Judges

Stanley Plumly
POETRY

Amy Hempel
FICTION

Terry Tempest Williams
CREATIVE NONFICTION